Genre Persuasive Text

Essential Question
How can starting a business help others?

D1738897

START SMALL
THINK BIG

BY JULIA WALL

Chapter 1

SMALL BEGINNINGS

It takes a great idea to start a business. Then it takes time, energy, and courage.

Entrepreneurs are people who start businesses. They get ideas by looking for something that people need or want. Entrepreneurs must convince people that their ideas are good. They must also get money to start their businesses.

Entrepreneurs have setbacks. People may say their enterprises won't work. But when entrepreneurs succeed, they can make a big difference.

Lila and DeWitt Wallace took big risks to start a new business.

DeWitt Wallace

Lila Wallace

In 1919, DeWitt Wallace and Lila Wallace had an idea for a magazine called *Reader's Digest*. The magazine had short articles to inform and entertain people. DeWitt had a process of finding nonfiction articles that had already been published. DeWitt revised the articles to make them shorter. Then he put the revised articles into the magazine.

DeWitt Wallace sent 200 copies of the magazine to publishers. He hoped a publisher would publish it.

The publishers didn't think the magazine was a good idea. But the Wallaces <u>believed in</u> their idea. They published and sold the magazine themselves.

They borrowed money and raised funds to print 5,000 copies of the first *Reader's Digest* in 1922.

The magazine was an instant success. In 1926, twenty thousand copies were sold by mail in the United States. In 1929, *Reader's Digest* was sold on newsstands as well as by mail.

> **In Other Words**
> had confidence in.
> En español, *believed in*
> quiere decir *creyeronen*.

magazine covers

Reader's Digest still sells millions of copies today.

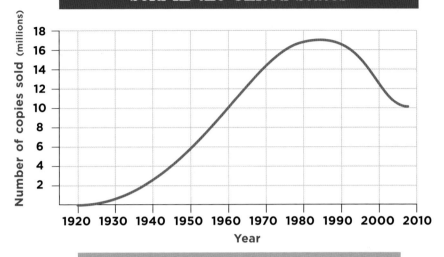

Number of Copies of *Reader's Digest* Sold in the United States

Number of copies sold (millions)

18
16
14
12
10
8
6
4
2

1920 1930 1940 1950 1960 1970 1980 1990 2000 2010

Year

In 2010, *Reader's Digest* began publishing ten times a year insted of twelve. This meant that fewer copies were printed.

The Wallaces wanted to help their **community**. They donated money to The Juilliard School, a **performing arts** school in New York City.

The Wallaces died in the early 1980s. They left donations to organizations that support schools and arts programs. Today *Reader's Digest* is one of the most popular magazines in the world.

STOP AND CHECK

How did the Wallaces start their magazine?

Chapter 2

WHAT A PERFORMANCE!

In the 1950s, a dancer named Alvin Ailey had a great idea. Ailey wanted people to dance.

Alvin Ailey was born in Rogers, Texas, in 1931. There were no jobs in Rogers, so Ailey and his mother moved often. <u>When</u> Ailey was 11 years old, he and his mother moved to Los Angeles.

Language Detective	<u>When</u> is a relative adverb. What kind of clause is it part of?

America in the 1930s

During the Great Depression in the 1930s, banks and businesses closed. As a result, millions of people lost their jobs and homes.

At this time, African Americans didn't have the same rights as white people. Many did not receive as good an education as white people. This made it difficult to get work. Many African Americans moved to find work.

In Los Angeles, Ailey became interested in dance. He trained with a dance teacher named Lester Horton.

In the early 1950s, Ailey moved to New York City. He studied ballet, modern dance, and acting. He also worked as a dancer and actor.

In 1958, Ailey formed the Alvin Ailey American Dance Theater. He used dance to show <u>what it was like to be</u> African American. The company's first major performance was an innovative ballet called *Blues Suite*.

> **In Other Words** the characteristics of being.
> En español, *what it was like to be* quiere decir *como era.*

Alvin Ailey's ballet *Blues Suite* combined styles from modern dance, jazz, ballet, and African dance.

dancers

stage

7

Alvin Ailey helped many people to learn to dance.

Ailey's childhood experiences inspired *Blues Suite*. Ailey's most famous dance routine, *Revelations*, tells the story of Ailey's childhood in Texas.

The Alvin Ailey American Dance Theater has performed in concerts and on TV.

Ailey started education programs for children. The programs taught dance and life skills, such as teamwork. Alvin Ailey died in 1989, but his dance company continues to thrive.

STOP AND CHECK

Why did Alvin Ailey form a dance company?

Chapter 3

HELPING OTHERS

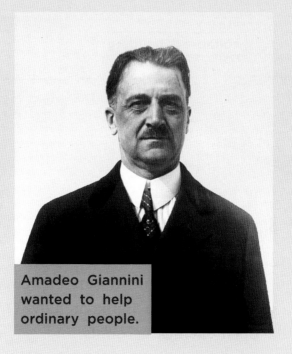

Amadeo Giannini wanted to help ordinary people.

Amadeo Giannini was a compassionate person. He helped others by starting a business.

Before the 1900s, banks loaned money to wealthy people and businesses.

The banks didn't want customers who were immigrants, like Giannini's parents. Giannini borrowed money from friends and started his own bank.

Many buildings collapsed during an earthquake in San Francisco in 1906.

collapsed building

Giannini opened his bank in San Francisco in 1904. Giannini called it the Bank of Italy. Ordinary people could open savings accounts and get loans. Giannini loaned money to farmers, laborers, and store owners. Many of them were immigrants, too.

Giannini's undertaking was successful. In a year, the Bank of Italy had several thousand customers.

In 1906, an earthquake destroyed much of San Francisco and the bank building. Giannini continued to operate his bank on the street. He loaned money to help businesses rebuild after the earthquake.

Giannini opened Bank of Italy offices across California. He bought other banks. In 1930, Giannini changed the bank's name to the Bank of America.

In 1932, the Bank of America provided money to help build the Golden Gate Bridge in San Francisco. Without the bank's money, construction of the bridge might not have begun.

STOP AND CHECK

What inspired Giannini to start the Bank of Italy?

Before the Golden Gate Bridge was built, people traveled by ferry across San Francisco Bay.

Golden Gate Bridge

San Francisco Bay

David Forman/Image Source

Chapter 4

A SMART INVENTOR

Kavita Shukla was 13 years old when she invented the Smart Lid. This invention keeps dangerous chemicals safe in laboratories.

The Smart Lid has an alarm that sounds when a container is open or leaking. Kavita got the idea <u>when</u> her mom forgot to put the gas cap on her car.

Kavita's next invention came from drinking polluted water in India. Her grandmother gave Kavita a mixture of spices so she would not get sick. The spices worked.

Language Detective	<u>When</u> is a subordinating conjunction. What is the dependent clause?

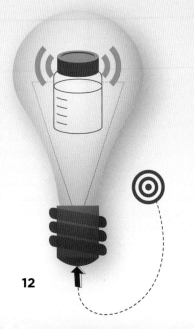

Kavita Shukla has won several awards for her inventions.

Kavita wondered if some of the spices could also preserve food. She discovered that food wrapped in paper treated with the spices lasts longer than food in regular packaging. The spiced paper also decomposes in the trash.

Now Kavita has a business that sells the paper she created. Kavita believes her invention can help more people eat fresh food.

Helping Communities Grow

Businesses are good for communities. They create jobs and help to develop an area. Many businesses also help the community. They take part in community events, such as festivals.

Communities should encourage new businesses. New businesses are the best way to help communities grow.

Bill Gates (right) started Microsoft when he was a teenager. He and his wife, Melinda (center), have given around $26 billion to good causes.

You read about entrepreneurs who took risks to start something new. Entrepreneurs work hard to make their ideas succeed. They often help their communities.

So look around you for new ideas. You could be an exceptional entrepreneur who starts small, thinks big, and helps your community, too.

STOP AND CHECK

How did Kavita get ideas for her inventions?

Respond to Reading

Summarize

Use important details to summarize *Start Small, Think Big*. Your graphic organizer may help you.

Main Idea
Detail
Detail
Detail

Text Evidence

1. What features of a persuasive text can you find in "Helping Communities Grow" on page 13? GENRE

2. Reread Chapter 2. What is the main idea? What are the key details that support it? MAIN IDEA AND KEY DETAILS

3. The word *invention* on page 12 includes the suffix *-ion*. This suffix changes a verb into a noun. What is the meaning of *invention*? SUFFIXES

4. Choose one entrepreneur from *Start Small, Think Big* and write about how the entrepreneur was able to help others. Use details from the text in your answer. WRITE ABOUT READING

Compare Texts

Read about how you can use your own money to help yourself and others.

Spending and Saving

What do you do with money? Do you spend it? Do you **deposit** it in a savings account?

It can be fun to buy things you want, such as a book or a game. It's a smart idea to save money. You may want to use the money to help others.

It might take a few weeks to save money to buy things, such as a T-shirt. It might take months for other things, such as a new bike. You need a savings plan to reach your goal.

To reach your goal, you can set up a **budget**. A budget helps you plan what you will save and what you will spend.

Setting Up a Budget

1. Calculate the amount of money you receive each week, such as your allowance or money for doing chores.

2. List the things that you buy every week and calculate the total amount you spend.

3. Subtract the money you spend from the money you receive. Figure out how much you can save each week.

4. Determine how long it will take you to save enough money to reach your goal.

Money Received	
Allowance	$10
Extra Chores	$8
TOTAL	**$18**
Money Spent	
Games and Toys	$3
School Supplies	$10
Donation	$2
TOTAL	**$15**
MONEY SAVED = $3	

You can make a chart like this to check your budget each week. The less you spend, the more you save. You can do many things with the money you save. You might start a business.

Make Connections

How can setting a budget allow you to help others? ESSENTIAL QUESTION

Why do you think the people who started businesses in *Start Small, Think Big* helped others? What kind of organization would you support if you were an entrepreneur? TEXT TO TEXT

Glossary

budget a plan of spending and saving *(page 17)*

community people who live in the same area *(page 5)*

deposit put money into a bank account *(page 16)*

entrepreneurs people who start their own businesses
(page 2)

performing arts activities such as dance, music, and
drama that are performed in front of an audience
(page 5)

Index

Focus on
Social Studies

Purpose To understand how a plan can help you raise money to help others

Procedure

Step 1 ▶ With a partner or group, brainstorm organizations in your community that you would like to support.

Step 2 ▶ Work with a group to plan an event to raise money for the organization, such as a bake sale, a theme night, or a fun run. You might choose an activity that takes place over a period of weeks.

Step 3 ▶ Figure out how much money you'll need to raise to reach your goal and how much time you'll realistically need to reach it.

Step 4 ▶ Now make a plan to raise the money. What will you need to do? Who will do the different tasks? What will it cost?